TABLE OF CONTENTS

About The Author

My name is Kelley Harris. I was born in Buford, GA. I am a Cook, Gastronomist, and a Social Media Influencer. When I was seven years old my life's ambition was to become a cook like my mom. My mom absolutely loved to cook. She spent most of her time in the kitchen where she would cook up all these savory dishes and I was right there with her. I soon picked up on some techniques that made me fall in love with the art of cooking. My mom would always say that people eat with their eyes first. Presentation is everything! The food that she cooked was always made with love and it was delicious. As an adult, I followed in my mother's footsteps. I started creating my own recipes. I became a food blogger and created my own cooking channel on social media. When I am in the kitchen, I can still feel the presents of my mom. Although she has been gone for many years, she is still in the kitchen with me. My mom is the reason why I fell in love with cooking but after doing some extensive soul-searching, I realized that what I loved most was seeing my family eating, laughing, and spending time together. It was the food that brought us together, but most importantly it was about family and fun.

I love you mom!

2 c. self-rising flour
1/3 c. plus 2 Tbsp. (cold) butter plus a
little extra to coat the pan.
1 c. cheddar cheese
1 c. milk
1/4 c. melted butter
1/2 tsp. garlic powder
1 tsp. parsley

Cheddar Biscuits

In a medium bowl add the flour, butter, cheddar cheese, and milk. Go ahead and give it a mix, but do not over-mix! Mix just until the batter comes together. The batter should look sticky. Grab a medium cast-iron pan. Coat the bottom with a little butter. Take a small ice cream scoop and scoop the batter onto the cast iron pan. Do not space the biscuits out. Place them right next to each other. They will grow together. You will have to pull them apart, but they will be super soft on the inside. Place them in a 375 degrees oven for about twenty minutes or until they are nice and brown. Remove them from the oven. Now prepare your herb butter topping. In a small bowl mix together the melted butter, garlic powder, and parsley, then use a food brush to spread the butter over the top of the biscuits. Do this while they are hot. Now it's time to dig in!

Cajun Shrimp & Grits

2 c. water
1/2 c. whole milk
1/2 c. grits
1/3 c. butter
1 tbs. olive oil
3 links andouille sausage
1/2 onion (chopped)
1 tsp. old bay seasoning
1 tsp. creole seasoning
1 tsp. cajun seasoning
1 tsp. garlic powder
1 tsp. onion powder

1 tsp. paprika
1 tsp. thyme
1 tsp. rosemary
1 tsp. Parsley
1 lb. lg shrimp (peeled & deveined
1 tbs. parsley
1/4 c. cream corn
1/4 c. cheddar jack cheese
1/3 c. smoked gouda

Let's start off with the grits. In a medium pot set to medium heat add water, milk, and the grits. When it comes to a boil, add the butter. Place the lid on and reduce the heat to medium-low. Check back occasionally to make sure that it is not sticking, and doesn't get too thick, add more water if necessary. In a separate pan set to medium heat, add the olive oil and the andouille sausage and let it cook for four minutes until the sausage turns brown on all sides, then add in the onions. Cook the onions until they become translucent. Remove the sausage and onion from the pan, and set aside. Mix all the seasonings together in a small bowl. Season the shrimp with one-half of the seasoning and reserve the rest for later. Add the shrimp to the same pan that you cooked the sausage in. Cook for about three minutes until they turn pink. DO NOT overcook! Add the parsley then remove the shrimp from the pan. Your grits should be done now. Add in the cheese and corn, then mix it all in. When the cheese is all melted remove it from the heat. Now in the same pan that you cooked the shrimp in, add the butter and flour. Cook on medium heat until the flour turns brown, then add in the chicken broth. Keep stirring until it starts to thicken up and turn into gravy. Next, add the seasoning that you reserved and mix well. Now it's time to plate it up. Grits on the bottom. Next, the shrimp then top with gravy. Now Devour!

Sweet & Sour Chicken

2 chicken breasts (cut into chunks)
I tsp. salt
I tsp. white pepper
I c. flour
I tbsp. corn starch
I tsp. baking powder
1/2 tsp. salt
I egg white
1/4 c. cold water
1/2 c. ketchup
1/2 c. sugar
2 tbsp. rice vinegar
I tsp. dark soy sauce
I tbsp. oil
I bell pepper chopped
I red pepper chopped
I clove fresh garlic (chopped)
1/2 c. pineapple tidbits
4 c. pineapple juice (reserved from the tidbits).

Let's start off with the chicken breast. Add the chicken to a medium bowl, add the salt and pepper then set it aside. In a separate bowl add the flour, cornstarch, baking powder, salt, egg whites, and cold water. Grab another bowl and add the ketchup, sugar, rice vinegar, and dark soy sauce. Drain the juice from the pineapples and add the juice to this red sauce and set the pineapples aside. Add cooking oil to a large pot and pre-heat to 350 degrees. Dip your chicken into the wet flour batter one at a time then add it to the oil. Fill the pot with the chicken to about half full. Cook each batch of chicken for about 4 to 5 minutes then remove it from the oil. Crank the oil temperature up to 375 degrees, then add your chicken back in. Cook the chicken for an additional 2 to 3 minutes, or until the chicken is golden brown and extra crispy. Remove the chicken from the pot and let it drain on a paper towel. While your chicken is draining grab another large pan and add I tbsp of oil. When the oil is heated, add in the bell peppers and red peppers. Cook for about 2 minutes then add in the garlic. Cook the garlic for an additional minute then add in the pineapples. Add the chicken to the pan with the bell peppers, onions, and pineapples. Then pour the red sauce on top. Now it's time to grub!

5.

Teriyaki Oven Roasted Brussel Sprouts

1 lb. Brussel Sprouts
1 tbsp. sesame oil
1 tsp. salt
1 tsp. white pepper
1 tsp. garlic powder
1 tbsp. Teriyaki sauce
2 tsp. sugar
1 tbs. toasted sesame seeds

Cut the brussels sprouts in half. Place them into a large bowl. Add in the sesame oil, salt, pepper, garlic powder, teriyaki sauce, and sugar. Mix them all together. Place the sprouts on a baking sheet lined with parchment paper or foil. Cook in a 375 degrees oven for about 25 minutes or until tender. Remove them from the oven, and add your toasted sesame seeds. Now Enjoy!

Japanese Clear Soup

1 tbs. sesame oil
1 onion cut into chunks
2 whole carrots cut into chunks
2 cloves garlic (chopped)
1 c. chicken broth
1 c. beef broth
1 c. water
1 tbs. ginger paste
1 tbs. lemongrass paste
1/4 c. thinly sliced scallions
1 c. thinly sliced mushrooms

In a large pot set to medium heat, add onions, carrots, and garlic. Cook for about 3 to 4 minutes then add in the chicken broth, beef broth, and water. Next, add the ginger paste and the lemongrass paste. Bring it to a boil. Then turn it down to simmer. Let it simmer for about an hour. Take a wooden spoon and skim the skin from the top of the broth, then take a strainer and strain the broth from the veggies. The broth should be clear. Now, add the broth to a bowl and add in your thin slices of mushroom and scallions. Enjoy this soup with some fried tortilla chips.
Now Enjoy!

Jalapeno Hushpuppies

1 c. self-rising corn meal
1/2 c. flour
1/4 c. onions (chopped)
2 tbsp. jalapenos (chopped)
1/2 c. cream style corn
1 egg
1/4 c. water
Oil for frying

In a medium bowl add the corn meal, flour, onions, jalapenos, and corn, and mix well. Let it sit to rise for about 10 minutes. Heat the oil in a large pot to 325 degrees. Take a small scoop and scoop the batter into the hot oil. Fill the pot til about half full. Let the hushpuppies cook for about 4 to 5 minutes until they are golden brown. Place them on a paper towel to drain. Get you some sweet chili sauce. Now enjoy!

Cheesy Corn

I tbs. butter
I tbs. fresh garlic chopped
2 c. frozen or canned whole kernel corn (drained)
salt & pepper to taste
4 oz. cream cheese
I c. queso cheese
I c. sharp cheddar cheese
1/2 c. half & half
1/2 tsp. red pepper flakes
I tsp. chives
1/2 tsp. paprika

In a pan set to medium heat add the butter and garlic. Let it cook for about I to 2 minutes then add in the corn. Next, add the salt and pepper. When the corn starts to heat up add in the cream cheese, queso cheese, and cheddar cheese. When the cheese starts to melt add in the half and half. Let it continue to cook until all of the cheese has melted completely. Sprinkle the top with red pepper flakes and chives. Plate it up and add on more chives if you like.
Now enjoy!

9.

Roasted Chicken

2 to 4 lb. chicken
I cup Cajun injection creole butter
I tbsp. fresh thyme
I tbsp. fresh rosemary
I tbs. olive oil
I clove garlic paste
2 tbsp. creole butter

Start off by cleaning the chicken and remove the inside bag of giblets and neck. Take a paper towel and dry the whole chicken off. Place the chicken on a baking sheet. Inject the cajun creole butter into the chicken, making sure you inject the chicken under the legs, wings, and breast in several places. In a small bowl add the thyme, rosemary, olive oil, garlic paste, and creole butter. Rub the mixture all over the outside of the chicken. Place the chicken in a 425 degrees oven or a 375 degrees air fryer uncovered. Roast the chicken for 45 to 55 min or until the juices run clear. You can also test it with a food thermometer. The internal temperature should be 165 degrees F. Remove the chicken and cover it with foil and let the chicken rest for 15 minutes. Now enjoy!

Country Collard Greens

1 bunch of fresh collard greens
1 pack smoked turkey wings
1 tbsp. olive oil
1 onion (chopped)
3 cloves garlic (chopped)
4 c. chicken stock
1 c. water
1 serrano pepper (chopped)
1 tsp. garlic powder
1 tsp. onion powder
salt and pepper to taste

TO CLEAN
Bowl Of Water
1 tbsp. apple cider Vinegar
1 tsp. baking soda

Start off by triple washing the collard greens to clean them. I like to wash my collard greens with apple cider vinegar and baking soda. Use two bowls, and fill them with water, baking soda, and vinegar. Wash the collard greens three to four times or until you see no more grit or sand. Refill the bowls with fresh water, vinegar, and baking soda each time. When the collards are clean they are ready to cook. In a large pot preheat the oil to medium heat then add in the onions. Cook the onions until they are translucent for three minutes, then add in the garlic. Wait for another minute then add in the collard greens. Pour in the chicken stock and water. Make sure you don't overfill the pot or it will boil over when it gets hot. Place the smoked turkey on top of the greens then place the lid on the pot. Cook for one hour. After the first hour add the chopped serrano pepper, garlic powder, and onion powder. Mix it all in and then place the lid back on the pot. Check back every hour to make sure that the smoked turkey falls off the bone. This should happen after about three hours. When the meat has fallen off the bone, remove the bones from the collard greens and discard them. Your greens are all done just add in some salt and pepper.
Don't forget the cornbread...
Now enjoy!

11.

Mr. Albert Lee Harris (Poppy)

I was blessed to be able to taste Poppy's wings before I actually had a chance to meet him. It was the year 1999 I was on a date with his son, who is now my husband Josh Harris. One night I pulled into his parent's driveway and Josh walked out of the house with one of those big old white styrofoam cups. As he got into the car I could smell the aroma of the spices coming from the hot sauce. The smell was mesmerizing! I asked him what in the world did he have in that cup. His reply to me was Poppy Wings. I had no idea what Poppy wings were at that time. He told me that they were his dad's wings. When Poppy made his wings Josh and his brother would fill their cups up with the wings before they headed out to the clubs. I thought that was kind of cool, but the wings were smelling so good that I just had to have a taste. To make a long story short Josh and I sat in that driveway and tore those wings up. He ended up going back into the house to get some more. I could not wait to meet Poppy because I had to meet the man behind those delicious wings. After I got a chance to know him. It took me some time to get him to trust me with his wing recipe and I was blessed to receive it. To this day I have yet to find a wing recipe as good as his. My family asks me often to make Poppy's Wings. He is in a better place now but, I know he is smiling over us as we are still eating his wings.

SIP Poppy. I love you and miss you so very much!

Poppy Wings

1 tbsp. seasoned salt
24 wing parts
1 c. Franks hot sauce
1/2 c. Moores hot sauce
1/2 tsp. paprika
1/2 tsp. chili powder
1 tsp. garlic powder
1 tsp. onion powder
1 tsp. lemon pepper
1 c. butter
Parsley for garnish
oil for frying

Albert Lee Harris

In a crock pot set to high heat add the Franks hot sauce, Moores hot sauce, paprika, chili powder, garlic powder, onion powder, lemon pepper, and butter, and mix well. Then place the lid on. Heat oil in a large pot or deep fryer to 375 degrees. While the oil is heating up, clean the chicken, place it in a large bowl add the seasoned salt and mix well. Next, add the seasoned chicken to the hot oil and cook for 15 to 20 minutes until golden brown. Do not overfill the deep fryer or pot. It may take several batches to completely fry all of the chicken. When the chicken is done add the chicken to the crock pot. Mix the chicken in the sauce and then place the lid on. Set the crock pot to low and let the chicken simmer for about 15 to 20 minutes. You are about to be sucking on the bone, I promise! Garnish with parsley. Now enjoy!

13.

Fruity Salmon Salad

FOR THE SALMON
3 salmon steak
1/4 tsp. garlic powder
1/4 tsp. onion powder
1/4 tsp. old bay
1/4 tsp. thyme
1/4 tsp. rosemary
2 tbsp. olive oil

SALAD TOPPINGS
Salad mix of your choice
tomatoes
cucumbers
red onion
blackberries
blueberries
raspberries
strawberries
boiled eggs

Pour I tbsp of the oil over the front and back of the salmon. Add all of the seasonings into a small bowl and mix well. Rub the seasonings on both sides of the salmon. In a medium pan set to medium heat add the remaining oil and salmon. Cook salmon on each side for about 4 minutes. Remove the salmon from the stove and place it in a 375 degrees oven for an additional 3 minutes. Remove the salmon from the oven and let it cool. While the salmon is cooling down start making your salad. Add all of the ingredients listed to a bowl. You can use as much of each item as you like. This is your salad! I like to top my salad with a little red wine vinegar, lemon juice, and olive oil. You can use whatever salad dressing you like. Now to eat and enjoy!

IN LOVING MEMORY

Mom

Dad

KayKay

BY
KELLEY WANSLEY HARRIS

Asian Sticky Wings

1 lb. chicken wing sections
1 tsp. seasoned salt
1 tsp. garlic powder
1 tsp. onion powder
1 tbsp. corn starch
1 tbs. sesame oil
1 tsp. garlic paste
1 tsp. ginger paste

1 tsp. rice Asian vinegar
1/4 c. chili sauce
2 tbsp. honey
1/4 c. brown sugar
1 tbsp. dark soy sauce
oil for frying
green onions for topping

Preheat the oil in a deep fryer or large pot to 375 degrees. Clean the chicken then place the sections into a large bowl. Add in the seasoned salt, garlic powder, onion powder, and cornstarch, and mix it all together. When the temperature has reached 375 degrees add in the chicken. (This can also be done by placing the chicken on a baking sheet and adding it to a 425 degrees oven or a 375 degrees air fryer) Cook for 20 to 25 minutes or until golden brown. While the chicken is cooking go ahead and make the sauce. In a medium bowl mix together the sesame oil, garlic paste, ginger paste, rice vinegar, chili sauce, brown sugar, soy sauce, and dark soy sauce, and mix it well. Pour the sauce into a medium wok or saucepan and set it to medium heat. Let it cook until it thickens. When the chicken is done add the chicken to the sauce and mix well. Make sure you cover all of the chicken with the sauce. Turn the heat off, then remove it from the stove. Go ahead and grab yourself a plate, and add some rice with the wings. Top it off with some green onions and enjoy!

16.

Focaccia Bread

The Dough
4 c. bread flour
I pack of instant yeast
I tbs. kosher salt

2 c. warm water
1/4 c. olive oil

Topping
I tbs. Rosemary
Fresh thinly sliced garlic
Sea Salt

In a large bowl add flour, salt, and yeast. Using a rubber spatula mix together until there is no more liquid. Knee the dough for just a few minutes in the bowl and form a ball. Pour I tbsp of oil over the dough making sure that you cover it all the way around. Cover the bowl with plastic wrap and place it in the refrigerator for 12 hours While the dough is in the refrigerator get yourself a baking sheet. Grease the baking sheet with oil or butter you can also use parchment paper. After 12 hours place the dough on a greased baking sheet or parchment paper. Deflate the dough and let it rest in the pan for an additional 4 hours. After 4 hours the dough should have risen a second time, now it's time to dimple the dough. Grease your hands with some of the olive oil and then pour the rest of the oil over the dough. Start dimpling the dough with your fingers until you have covered it all. Top with thin slices of garlic, sprinkles of rosemary, and sea salt. Place it in a 425 degrees oven and cook for 25 to 30 minutes or until it is golden brown. Remove from the oven and give it a try while it's hot. Enjoy!

Chicken & Corn Chowder

1/2 stick butter
1 onion chopped
1 red pepper chopped
1 yellow pepper chopped
3 cloves garlic
3 large potatoes chopped
3 chicken breasts chopped
2 c. fresh or canned corn
4 c. chicken stock
1 tsp. garlic powder
1 tsp. onion powder
1 tsp. thyme
1 tsp. salt
1 tsp. pepper
2 bay leaves
1 c. heavy cream
1 tbsp. cornstarch
1 tbsp. water
1 tbsp. parsley

In a large pot set to medium heat add in the butter and let it melt. Then add in the onion, red peppers, yellow peppers, garlic, potatoes, chicken, corn, and chicken stock. Mix well, and let it cook for about 8 minutes. Add in the garlic powder, onion powder, thyme, salt, pepper, and bay leaves. Let it cook for an additional 10 minutes then reduce the heat to a simmer. Add in the heavy cream and mix well. In a small bowl add the cornstarch and the water and mix it well. This is called a slurry. It is used to thicken up gravy, soups, and sauces. Pour it into the chowder and stir it until it starts to thicken up. Lastly, add the parsley. Let it simmer for another five minutes. Now get some fresh croissants and enjoy!

Chicken & Waffles

4 chicken breasts
(split into halves)
Oil for frying

WET BATTER
1/2 c. self-rising flour
1 tsp. seasoned salt
1 tsp. garlic powder
1 tsp. onion powder
1 tsp. Creole seasoning
1 tsp. lemon pepper
seasoning
1/2 c. water

DRY BATTER
1 c. self-rising flour
1 tsp. seasoned salt
1 tsp. garlic powder
1 tsp. onion powder
1 tsp. Creole seasoning
1 tsp. lemon pepper
seasoning

THE WAFFLE
1 1/2 c. self-rising flour
1/4 tsp. salt
1 tbsp. sugar
1 c. milk
2 eggs
1/2 tsp. vanilla
1/3 c. butter (melted)

Preheat a deep fryer or a large pot of oil to 350 degrees. In a large bowl mix together the flour, all of the seasonings, and the water. This will be the wet batter. Add the chicken to this wet batter. Make sure you cover it well. Grab a separate large bowl and mix together the flour and all of the seasonings for the dry batter. Take the wet battered chicken and drop each piece into the dry batter and then place it into the deep-fryer or pot. Fry for 11 to 15 minutes until the chicken is golden brown and crispy. Remove the chicken from the deep fryer and place it on a paper towel to drain off the excess grease. While the chicken is resting you can start on your waffles. In a medium bowl mix together the flour, salt, and sugar. In a separate medium bowl mix together the milk, eggs, and vanilla. Pour the wet mixture into the dry mixture and mix it well. The batter should be smooth like a pancake mix. Add in the butter slowly making sure to mix it all in. Let the waffle batter rest for ten minutes before cooking. Heat up your waffle maker and spray it with some cooking spray, then add in the batter. Cook the waffle until it is golden brown, about 2 minutes. Remove the waffle and add it to a plate. Put the chicken on top of your waffle and pour on some of your favorite syrup. Now enjoy!

19.

Squash & Zucchini Cassarole

CORN BREAD	I medium pan of prepared	6 large eggs
2 c. corn meal	regular cornbread	2 c.chicken stock
2 eggs	I medium pan of prepared	I tsp. onion powder
I c. butter milk	jiffy cornbread.	I tsp.garlic powder
I/2 c. water	I stick butter	I tsp. sage
I/3 c. Conola oil	2 large squashes sliced into	I tsp. thyme
(plus more for the pan)	pieces	I tsp. salt
	2 large zucchinis sliced into	I tsp. white pepper
THE JIFFY CORN BREAD	pieces	2 c. cheddar cheese
2 pkg of Jiffy Muffin Mix	I large onion sliced into	I c. smoked gouda
2 eggs	pieces	
2/3 c. milk		
butter for pan		

Start with the regular cornbread first. Add the corn meal, eggs, buttermilk, and oil, to a medium bowl and mix well. Add about a tablespoon of oil into a cast iron pan, then take your fingers and spread it around until you have fully covered the pan. Pour the batter into the cast iron pan then place it in a 350 degrees oven for about 25 to 30 minutes until it is golden brown. Remove it from the oven and let it rest. Now for the jiffy cornbread. Take two packages of jiffy muffin mix, 2 eggs, and 2/3 cups of milk and add it to a bowl, and mix it all together. Take about a tablespoon of butter and spread it around a medium cast-iron pan until it is fully covered then pour in the Jiffy batter. Cook for 25 minutes until golden brown, then remove it from the oven and let it rest. Take both pans of cornbread, add them to a large bowl, and mash it all together. In a large skillet on medium heat add the butter, zucchini, squash, and onions. Cook until tender about 4 minutes then pour it into the bowl with the cornbread. Add in the eggs, chicken stock, and all of the seasonings, then take a spatula and mix it all together. Mix in one cup of the cheddar cheese and all of the gouda cheese. Pour the batter into a baking dish then add the remaining cheddar cheese on top. Bake in a 350 degrees oven for 25 to 30 minutes. Take a toothpick and insert it into the center. If it comes out clean, then it's done. Remove from the oven and let it rest for 15 minutes before eating Now Enjoy!

Country Butter Biscuits

2 c. self-rising flour
1 tbsp. sugar
1 stick salted butter
1 c. buttermilk
baking sheet for cooking
1 tbsp. butter
1/4 c. melted butter

Prepare a baking sheet by taking 1 tablespoon of butter and coating it. Now grab a large bowl and add in the flour, and sugar, and mix well. While the butter is still cold add it to the flour and sugar. Take your fingers and start mashing the butter into the flour until you have reached the consistency of cornmeal. Pour in the buttermilk, then mix until it is combined, do not over-mix. Overworking the dough will make the biscuits tough. When you are done mixing turn the dough out onto a floured surface. Flatten the dough until it is about 1 inch thick. Take a biscuit cutter and cut the biscuits out. Place the biscuits onto the baking sheet and put them into a 425 degrees oven for 12 to 15 minutes. Remove them from the oven and brush them with melted butter while they are hot. Now Enjoy!

Air-Fryer Ribs

I rack of ribs
I tbsp. Creole seasoning
Itbs. smoked paprika
I tbsp. chili powder
I tbsp. onion powder
I tbsp. garlic powder
I tbsp. dry mustard
1/4 c. brown sugar

Clean, wash, and remove the membrane from the back of the ribs. Next, take a small bowl, add all of the seasonings together, and mix well. Pour the seasonings onto the ribs. Take your hands and rub it all in, making sure you cover the entire ribs. Place the ribs onto an air-fryer rack, then place them into the air fryer, and set it to 375 degrees. After 25 minutes flip the ribs over then cook for additional 25 minutes. The internal temperature should be 170. Remove the ribs from the air-fryer and brush on some of your favorite BBQ sauce. Place it back in the air-fryer for another 5 minutes. Remove the ribs and let them rest for about 10 minutes then enjoy

Country Fried Okra

I lb. okra pods
I c. cornmeal
1/4 c. all-purpose flour
I tsp. salt.
I tsp. pepper
I tsp. creole seasoning
(plus more for topping)
I egg
1/2 c. buttermilk

Preheat a deep fryer or large pot to 350 degrees. Cut the stems and tips off of the okra and discard them, then cut the rest of the okra into 1/2-inch pieces. Get a large bowl and combine the corn meal, flour, salt, pepper, and creole seasoning. Get a separate bowl and mix together the egg and buttermilk. Place the okra into the wet mixture a couple of pieces at a time. Then add the pieces to the dry mixture. Once the okra is covered, add them to a baking sheet. Repeat this process until you have all of the okra covered. Add the okra to the deep fryer or pot. Cook for 7 or 8 minutes until the okra is golden brown. Remove the and place it on a paper towel to drain off the excess oil. Season with creole seasoning while it is hot. Now Enjoy!

23.

Seafood Gumbo

I pack of andouille sausages cut into chunks
1/2 c. vegetable oil
1/2 c. butter
I c. flour
I c. sweet onion
I c. green bell pepper
I c. red bell pepper
I c. yellow bell pepper
I c. celery
I c. green onion
4 cloves fresh garlic chopped
6 c. seafood stock
I c. beer
I tsp. old bay
I tsp. Creole seasoning
I tsp. onion powder
I tsp. garlic powder
I tsp. thyme
I tsp. gumbo file
2 bay leaves
I lb. large peeled and deveined shrimp
I 8oz. container of crab meat
2 c. fresh okra cut into chunks
I tsp. parsley

Start off with a large pot set to medium heat. Add in the sausage and cook until they are nice and brown about 5 minutes. Remove the sausage and set aside. In the same pot add the vegetable oil, butter, and flour. Stir continuously until it turns to a cocoa-brown color. It's going to take about 20 minutes for this to happen, so be patient. When it has reached the cocoa brown color add in all of your veggies and garlic. Cook for about 5 minutes, until the veggies are tender then add in the seafood stock and the beer. Let it come up to a boil and then add in all of the seasonings. Next, add the sausage, shrimp, crab meat, and okra. Let it cook for another ten minutes then reduce the heat to a simmer. Let it simmer for another ten minutes. Top it off with some parsley. Pair with some rice and Enjoy!

IT'S ME KELLZ
Special Thanks

KELLEY HARRIS

Kokeeta

Kadeem

I would like to give a very special thanks to my wonderful amazing and supportive husband Josh Harris. You are always encouraging me to shoot for the stars. I love you with every fiber of my being. I would also like to say thank you to my children and grandchildren for loving me and supporting me even when it doesn't make sense. Y'all are my everything and nothing works without yall. God has blessed me with an amazing family, and I will never take it for granted.
Love forever and Always
Mom 🖤

Joshua

Joshua

Drea

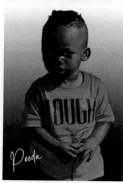

Pooda

Made in United States
Orlando, FL
12 October 2024

52459106R00015